Robert E. Lee

The eternal soul and spirit of an unconquerable South, Robert E. Lee magnificently portrayed the classic heroic role in the great American tragedy, The Brothers War. As the "Rebel General," he was a military genius. In the words of Winston Churchill he was "one of the greatest captains ever known to the annals of war." Other writers have praised him as "one of the greatest, if not the greatest soldier, who ever spoke the English language." The affection of his valiant barefoot and threadbare soldiers, even during times of calamity and near-starvation, bordered on godlike adoration. "Possibly his greatest weakness," it has been said, "was his extreme kindness and humility in dealing with subordinate officers who needed forceful and direct leadership."

Now, more than a hundred years after the Civil War, Lee is yet known mostly only as the "Rebel General" who somehow seems to have vanished into oblivion after the conflict. Bold and audacious with the fighting heart of a soldier, he was still courteous and pious as a human being. Even when the worst outrages were being perpetrated against the people of the states then in rebellion, Lee was never moved to retaliate in kind, even praying for his enemies. In his reluctant involvement in America's sectional conflict, he was essentially, strangely enough, a peacemaker at heart, quite advanced in his disbelief in slavery, secession, and war as a resolution of internal strife.

It was after the guns fell silent and the fighting was over that Lee made his most significant and most overlooked contributions to his country. As the magnificent symbol of the South's heritage, he stood taller than other men as a shining living example of magnanimity during all the bitterness of the "Age of Hate" and became an enduring symbol to the people of the South. Rising above all hostility, he led the vanguard in preaching forgiveness, nationalism, and the reuniting of a nation in heart and spirit that had been bloodily welded back together by the brute force of arms. In the wreckage of his own fortunes he advocated the rebuilding of a "New South," setting the example with his progressive program in education.

Once Lee is viewed as a simple man, an honorable man, a religious man committed to the life task he felt God had assigned him, he immediately becomes quite understandable and human as a man for all seasons with a message of eternal relevance for every generation of Americans. Through his innate nobility he not only breathed new life into a prostrate South, but helped bind the wounds of a bleeding nation at large.

The Lee homes at Arlington and Stratford, Virginia, as well as historic Appomattox Court House where Grant refused to take Lee's sword following his surrender, are today national shrines. In 1975, more than a hundred years later, the United States finally restored Lee's citizenship.

THE VIRGINIAN

Robert E. Lee was born early on a frosty morn on Jan. 19, 1807. Like his artistocratic Southern forebearers, he first saw the light of day in the stately family mansion "Stratford Hall" on the Potomac, midway between Washington and Richmond, in Westmoreland County, Virginia. Both sides of his family had spawned eminent members of Virgnia's aristocratic ruling class since early Colonial times, as well as some of the most outstanding figures of the American Revolution.

Robert Edward Lee was the fourth child of colorful Col. Henry Lee and Ann Hill Carter. His father, the dashing "Light Horse Harry" Lee, was a bold and brilliant cavalry leader during America's fight for independence. Author of the famous Congressional eulogy for his friend and fellow Virginian George Washington, Henry Lee had also been elected Governor of Virginia after the war, at that time the biggest, most populous, and most influential state in the four-year-old Union. Robert's mother was a Carter, a leading family in Colonial Virginia, and the daughter of one of Virginia's wealthiest planters. Although the Lees and the Carters had been leading lights in Virginia society since the early 1600's, it was not until 1793 at the magnificent June wedding at Shirley Plantation that these two great Virginia families became joined in marriage.

The Lees traced their genealogy back to Lee of Shropshire, England, whose lineage descended from a Twelfth Century Norman, Rayner de Lega (or de Le'). The Lees of Virginia traced their background to "the immigrant," Richard Lee the First, who planted in the Northern Neck in 1641. Landowner, planter, shipowner, merchant, Richard the First also became Secretary of State of the Virginia Colony at thirty-three.

When Robert E. Lee was born, only thirty years had elapsed since his kinsmen Francis Lightfoot Lee and Henry Lee had added their signatures to the Declaration of Independence authored by another famous Virginian Thomas Jefferson. The "Sage of Monticello" was just completing his second term as President, beginning the quarter-century reign of the Virginia Dynasty in Washington. By now, however, a cruel turn of fortune had cast glorious Stratford Hall into the deepening shadows of gloom and decay. "Light Horse Harry's" serious financial reverses had reduced the Lee family almost to a hand-to-mouth situation.

About the time of Robert's fourth birthday, the Lee's financial plight forced the family to abandon Stratford Hall and move into a small house in Alexandria, Virginia, just across the Potomac from the nation's capital. Here Robert went to the same church George Washington had. In this historic atmosphere the boy's ideas took shape in those early formative years.

As war with Britain loomed for the second time in a generation (The War of 1812), "Light Horse Harry" was reactivated as a major general. But through another bad stroke of fortune he was beaten up and left for dead by a bloodthirsty mob in Baltimore when he came to the aid of a publisher friend who had written antiwar editorials in his newspaper. Physically broken, his face permanently disfigured, his career ended, with the help of his friends, Madison and Monroe, he caught a ship to the Barbados to recover his health.

THE SON

Robert was fortunate in inheriting his father's strong body, driving energy, and fearless courage. But his dark brown hair and eyes and his mental cast were inherited from his mother.

His father gone, Robert's mother now became head of the family. Feeling the pinch, "Mrs. Genel Lee" had to stretch every penny to make ends meet. From his mother young Robert learned to practice self-denial, self-control, strict economy, and an almost ritualistic sense of order in everything he did. There was no money to buy him a saddle horse, but Robert still followed the fox hunts—on foot.

Nor was there money to send him to a plantation school with tutors, such as his forebearers attended. He learned his basic reading, spelling, grammar, writing, and arithmetic from his mother at home. He also spent long hours delving through his father's well-stocked library. Still Robert must have learned well, for he was well-prepared when he entered the new Alexandria Academy under the tutelage of a learned Irishman, William B. Leary.

When Robert was nine years old, both Stratford Hall and Shirley Plantation were restored to their days of grandeur by two of his kinsmen. He could feel its heroic history as he walked the hallowed halls of Stratford. Hadn't the Lees who signed the Declaration of Independence been born in the very same room he had?

'DISTINGUISHED CADET' WITHOUT DEMERIT

With no money to send the young man to a private university, Robert had little choice but to try for either the military or naval academies. When Lee applied for admission to West Point, he gave Westmoreland County, the site of Stratford Hall, and not Alexandria, as his residence, showing his identification with his aristocratic plantation background. His tutor Mr. Leary vouched for his "correct and gentlemanly deportment," giving the young man an excellent and glowing rating. Leary wrote, "In the various branches to which his attention has been applied I flatter myself that his information will be found adequate to the most sanguine expectations of his friends. With me he has read all the minor classics in addition to

Homer, Longinus, Tacitus, and Cicero. He is well-versed in arithmetic, algebra and Euclid."

Lee was seventeen in March of 1824 when the mail brought the announcement from Secretary of War John C. Calhoun of his appointment. Prophetically, the same batch of appointments included the name of a young man from Mississippi named Jefferson Davis. The names Lee and Davis would become inextricably linked in years to come.

Commandant of West Point at the time was Lt. Col. Sylvanus Thayer. Some of the cadets broke under his harsh discipline. But to cadet Lee the disciplined life by now had become second nature. Although Lee was never the top scholar in any subject, he was always near the top. Where he was outstanding was in the way in which he performed all his duties. He made the list of "Distinguished Cadets," and at the end of his first year was given the highest honor a fourth classman could attain when he was made cadet staff sergeant.

Arriving home for summer vacation at the end of his second year, Lee was saddened to find his mother an invalid. He dutifully waited on her and became her full-time nurse. Now twenty, the West Point cadet had developed into a magnificent physical image. Even then, Lee stood out to his companions because of his erect carriage and "manly beauty." With his enviable physical attributes he also combined dignity, grace, kindness, and sympathy—all tempered with a basic good humor. His composed expression, even at twenty, was described as neither warm nor austere.

In his last year at the military academy Lee won the first classman's ultimate recognition by being appointed Corps Adjutant, the highest honor a cadet could attain. He won this honor not as the best student in his class, but because of his excellent standing in all phases of academy life and his position of leadership among his fellow cadets. Lee was also the first cadet ever to be graduated from West Point without receiving a single demerit. Robert E. Lee was commissioned a Brevet Second Lieutenant of Engineers.

Fellow Virginian Joe Johnston later wrote of the impression Lee had made at West Point. "We had the same intimate associates who thought as I did. No other youth or man so united the qualities that win warm friendship and command high respect, for he was full of sympathy and kindness, genial and fond of gay conversation, even fun, while his correctness of demeanor and attention to all duties, personal and official, and a dignity as much a part of himself as the elegance of his person, gave him a superiority that everyone acknowledged in his heart."

General Erasmus D. Keyes, who later served with Lee during the Mexican War and became an opposing Federal general during the Civil War, was a fourth classman when Lee was Corps Adjutant. Keyes later wrote, "I doubt if he ever incited envy in any man. . . . All his accomplishments and alluring virtues appeared natural to him, and he was free from anxiety, distrust, and awkwardness that attend a sense of inferiority."

Yet the proud and shining new second lieutenant's homecoming was not a happy one. This time Lee found his mother lying in bed in the final stages of her terminal illness. Again, he instinctively became his dying mother's full-time nurse. He was at her bedside when she finally closed her eyes. The memory of this tragic moment remained with Lee for the rest of his life. Years later, while attending another funeral in the same house, he lingered for a moment at the doorway to the room in which his mother had died and whispered, "Forty years ago I stood in this room by my mother's deathbed. It seems now but yesterday."

LOVING HUSBAND AND FATHER

Lee's initial assignment was to Fort Pulaski, Georgia, where he served for seventeen months before he was transferred to Fort Monroe, Virginia, in 1831. On June 30, 1831 the twenty-four-year-old lieutenant married Mary Anne Randolph Custis at Arlington. His new wife was the daughter of a grandson of Martha Washington. Seven children were eventually born to this marriage, all three of Lee's sons later serving in the Confederate army. Two of them, George Washington Custis Lee and William Fitzhugh Lee, made major general.

On Sept. 16, when Mrs. Lee gave birth to her first child, Lee immediately became a loving father and proud parent, undoubtedly recollecting his own warm and loving childhood, his closeness to his own mother. With it all, however, the "old soldier" demanded and expected the strictest obedience. As his son Robert remarked, "I always knew it was impossible to disobey my father. I felt within me—I never knew why, but was perfectly sure—when he gave an order that it had to be obeyed."

'NAT TURNERS' REBELLION'

Two months following Lee's marriage, on Aug. 23, 1831 a sobering event took place in Southampton County. Considering himself the divinely inspired avenger of the oppressed, Nat Turner, a negro slave, killed his coachmaker master and the coachmaker's family in their sleep. Gathering momentum as it went, Turner's little band then went on a bloody rampage of terror. Fifty-six men, women, and children were violently murdered before Turner and his band were stopped. Turner received the benefit of a legal trial, was found guilty, and hanged.

The bloody slave rebellion compelled the General Assembly to reconvene. At the 1831 convention it was evident that a growing proportion of Virginians, Lee included, believed in emancipation, but could find no practical and economical solution for relocating the freed negroes in their original African homeland. Virginia had been attempting to solve this knotty problem since as early as 1801, when an Emancipation Society was founded. James Madison was National President of the National Colonization Society founded in 1816 for the purpose of transporting freed negroes to Liberia. And the eminent John Marshall was president of the active Virginia branch. But not even the most zealous emancipationist in Virginia advocated freeing the slaves and leaving the freed black men in Virginia.

(Lee, it should be noted here, emancipated the few slaves he inherited from his mother and owned no others. Stonewall Jackson, who conducted a Sunday School for negro children, purchased two slaves at their own request and allowed them to earn their freedom. J. B. Johnston and A. P. Hill never owned slaves and were opposed to slavery. Jeb Stuart owned only two slaves, but disposed of them long before the Civil War.)

ENGINEERING OFFICER

Advancement was very slow in the Engineers. From 1834 to 1837 Lt. Lee was attached to the office of U. S. Engineers in Washington, D. C. While in this assignment, he surveyed and defined the boundary between Ohio and Michigan. In 1836 only his wife's condition kept Lee from resigning his commission. To escape the monotony, in 1837 he requested the assignment of changing the course of the Mississippi River at St. Louis, even though he had no experience at all with engineering river projects. Objecting to Lee's slow and thorough analysis of the situation, the people demanded quick action. But Lee was not a man to be pushed by anyone. A young fellow officer who served there the first year with Lee remarked, "He was one with whom no one ever wished or ventured to take a liberty, though kind and generous to his subordinates, admired by all women, and respected by all men." If the criticism did get under Lee's skin, he never did show it. The only response Lee made to the criticism was, "They have a right to do as they wish with their own. I do not own the city. The government has sent me here as an officer of the army to do certain work. I shall do it."

For twelve long years, from age twenty-seven to thirty-nine, Lee endured the insufferable tedium. He did not make first lieutenant until 1836 and captain two years later. But this seemed to be the end of the line in his military career. Gone now was the image of the dashing young lieutenant of yesteryear. Yet Lee never lost his dignity, his composure, his self-control, his sense of humor. Nor did he ever swear, drink, chew tobacco, or smoke cigars.

SECTIONAL CONFLICT SURFACES

In April of 1841 thirty-four-year-old Capt. Lee was given the mission of repairing a fort on the North Carolina coast, following which he was assigned to Fort Hamilton, Brooklyn, where his mission was to study and update the coastal defenses guarding New York harbor. Lee was becoming an expert in fortifications.

The long-smoldering differences between the North and the South over the course the growing nation would follow in its expansion were now beginning to surface. Slavery was not the basic issue then or afterward. The financial and economic differences between the two sections of the country traced their roots to early Colonial times.

From the outset, the United States of America never did come to grips with the institution of slavery, facing it as a national instead of a sectional problem. (Slavery was not confined to the South alone.) While England and Mexico were working on practical steps for the emancipation of the negro slave, the South made the fatal strategic error of allowing the institution of slavery to become enmeshed with sectional politics. This was as long as forty years before the outbreak of the Civil War, in 1820, when Lee was only a boy and the country was divided into eleven so-called "slave states" and eleven so-called "free states."

CATCHES COMMANDING GENERAL'S EYE

Lee was now approaching his mid-thirties. The young lieutenant's dark sideburns now were gone, and he wore a sedate-looking moustache. The gloss was just beginning to fade from his shiny dark hair. And now he brushed his hair across his scalp from a low part and wore it long on both sides. Yet with his growing maturity Lee looked even more impressive. As described by a young artillery lieutenant at the time, "He was then about thirty-five years of age, as fine-looking a man as one would wish to see, a perfect figure and strikingly handosme, quiet and dignified in manner, of cheerful disposition, always pleasant and considerate. He seemed to be the perfect type of a gentleman."

In June of 1844 Lee was selected as one of a special commission of officers to supervise the final examinations at the military academy. It was during this fateful two-week period at West Point that Capt. Lee came in contact with General-in-Chief of the Army Winfield Scott. Lee must have made a lasting impression on the older man, then fifty-eight. In a few years, with the Mexican War then looming, General Scott would call Capt. Lee "the very best soldier I ever saw in the field."

MEXICAN WAR

In March of 1845 the Republic of Texas was annexed to the Union, and when Polk assumed the Presidency, acquisition of California established the country's east and west boundaries at the Atlantic and Pacific Oceans. Historically, the southern boundary of Texas had been the Nueces River. In the peace treaty establishing Texas independence the boundary was established farther south at the Rio Grande. The new boundary was later repudiated by Mexico, and the area between the two rivers became disputed territory. In May the United States declared war on Mexico for invading "American territory."

General Winfield Scott's campaign was brilliant. Given little more than half the troops he had requested, hampered by jealous subordinates, political appointee officers, and an incompetent administration in Washington, forced to live off the land and fight with captured ammunition, he nevertheless was able to march his army to Mexico City along the same route followed by Hernando Cortés three centuries earlier.

The Mexican War was already three months old when on Aug. 19 Capt. Lee received his orders. Scott had been preparing an armada to land at Vera Cruz, then move inland to Mexico City. He needed a good engineering officer. On Jan. 6, 1847 Scott wrote Lee's commanding officer, "Of the officers of Engineers, Topographical Engineers and Ordnance with you, or under your command, I propose to take only Capt. R. Lee of the first named corps."

On Apr. 15 Gen. Scott sent Capt. Lee on reconnaissance at the heavily fortified pass of Cerro Gordo. Working his way around the left flank of the strong Mexican positions, where he could observe the enemy flank and rear, Lee envisioned a strategic plan which could wipe out the entire enemy position and send the enemy reeling. Acting upon Lee's strategic reconnaissance, Scott was able to overrun Cerro Gordo. It was a brilliant operation in which a Capt. George B. McClellan and a Lt. Ulysses S. Grant also took part.

Capt. Raphael Semmes singled Lee out in his battle report, writing, "His talent for topography was peculiar. He seemed to receive impressions intuitively that cost other men much labor to acquire." Other commanders whose troops Lee had directed to their positions were also lavish in their praise. Even old "Fuss and Feathers" Scott himself cited Lee in his own report, stating, "I am impelled to make special mention of the services of Capt. R. E. Lee, Engineers. This officer, greatly distinguished at the siege of Vera Cruz, was again indefatigable during these operations in reconnaissance as daring and laborious and of the utmost value. Nor was he less conspicuous in planting batteries and in conducting columns to their stations under the heavy fire of the enemy."

As Scott's army approached Mexico City, Lee was responsible for reconnaissance and road-building. When his working parties came under fire, he ordered two light field batteries moved forward, one commanded by John Bankhead Magruder, a fellow Virginian who had been a year behind Lee at West Point. In Magruder's battery was another West Point trained Virginian, twenty-three-year-old Thomas J. (later "Stonewall") Jackson. An infantry officer named George B. McClellan also helped the artillerymen place their pieces.

When the Americans were cut off, caught in a Mexican trap, it was Capt. Lee, of all the others, who volunteered to take the dawn counterattack plans back to Gen. Scott. After their victory Gen. Persifor Smith reported, "In adverting to the conduct of the staff, I wish to record particularly my admiration of (Lee's) conduct. . . . His reconnaissances, though carried far beyond the bounds of prudence, were conducted with so much skill that their fruits were of the utmost value, the soundness of his judgment and personal daring being equally conspicuous."

'THE VERY BEST SOLDIER I EVER SAW IN THE FIELD'

Lee was promoted to brevet lieutenant colonel and Gen. Scott made him his special aide and acting chief of artillery, calling Lee "the very best soldier I ever saw in the field." The opportunity to work closely with the general-in-chief gave Lee invaluable military training at the top level of command. The deep and lasting impression made upon Lee was Scott's method of planning his battles strategically, talking out his decisions, but leaving the detailed tactical execution to the initiative of his field commanders.

In the storming of Chapultepec, Sept. 1, Lee directed the cannon fire on the Mexican defenders. But the Americans were also taking casualties. When a big, burly twenty-six-year-old lieutenant named James Longstreet was hit, a young Virginian named George Pickett took the battle flag out of his hand and rushed forward. When one gun of a supporting artillery section was knocked out of action, men and horses down, a grim-faced young artillery lieutenant named Thomas J. Jackson stood to his one remaining gun and kept it firing all by himself. Somewhere in the frantic action Lee took a light flesh wound, but he paid no attention to it. Weakened by loss of blood, Scott's "very best soldier" and "indefatiguable" aide finally toppled from the saddle.

The Mexican War was over and Lee was now promoted to brevet colonel. Returning to his home in Arlington, Virginia, on June 29, he was now one of the most famous soldiers in the United States Army. But once again the fearless combat hero was returned to duty in the Engineers Bureau in Washington as a member of the board of engineers for the Atlantic Coast defenses.

COMMANDANT OF WEST POINT

From 1852 to 1855 Lee served as Commandant of West Point where he got to know the budding young officers who would eventually be fighting beside and against him. Discipline was at a high level at the Point during Lee's tour of duty. But he was never the martinet. He was a natural leader of men, adding his distinctive brand of tolerance and humanity to his understanding of the human being inside the uniform. And once again, as he had himself when a cadet at West Point, he won the high respect and regard of the cadets.

Lee was even able to work cheerfully with then Secretary of War Jefferson Davis, no mean accomplishment, for former fellow-cadet Davis was never the easiest man in the world to get along with. Finally completing his assignment as superintendent of West Point, in April of 1855 Lee was ordered to take charge of his first field command, joining the new Second Cavalry as a lieutenant colonel, regular rank, at Jefferson Barracks, St. Louis.

POWER STRUGGLE COMES OUT IN OPEN

Now the big "slave states" were beginning to make the same talk of secession the New England states had made over the War of 1812. While most of the people of the land went on about their daily business, the extremists, both North and South, continued to pour fuel on the smoldering fires.

Six years of duty at Camp Cooper in west Texas followed for Lee. Here in this bleak, lonely, hot, and dusty outpost he read the newspaper accounts of President Pierce's warnings to the radical abolitionists in the North. "Extremes beget extremes," the President said. "Violent attack from the North finds its inevitable consequence in the growth of a spirit of angry defiance in the South."

Commenting on the President's admonitions in a letter to his wife, Lee expressed the attitude of the average humanistic Southerner who had been exposed to thè institution of slavery, writing, "The views of the President . . . of the systematic and progressive efforts of certain people in the North, to interfere with and change the domestic institutions of the South, are truthfully and faithfully expressed. The consequences and purposes of their plans are clearly set forth and they must also be aware that their object is both unlawful and entirely foreign to them and their duties; they are irresponsible and unaccountable; and (abolition) can only be accomplished by *them* through the agency of a Civil and Servile war.

"In this enlightened age there are few, I believe, but will acknowledge that slavery as an institution is immoral and a political evil in any country. It is useless to expatiate on its disadvantages. I think it a greater evil to the white man than to the black race, and while my feelings are strongly enlisted in behalf of the latter, my sympathies are more for the former. The blacks are immeasurably better off here than in Africa, morally, socially, and physically. The painful discipline they are undergoing is necessary for their instruction as a race, and I hope will prepare and lead them to better things. How long this subjugation may be necessary is known and ordered by a Wise and Merciful Providence. Their emancipation will sooner result from the mild and melting influence of Christiantity than the storms and tempests of fiery controversy. This influence, though slow, is sure."

Never the blind adherent to any faction, Lee disapproved as much of the secessionist attitude of the slave interests in the Lower South as the interference of the Northern zealots in other states' affairs.

On Oct. 21, 1857 Lee was suddenly called home to Arlington. His father-in-law Washington Custis was dead, and his wife was the heiress of the Arlington estate. Lee returned home to hope to comfort his wife over the death of her father. But when he entered the family sitting room at Arlington, he was shocked to find her badly crippled with arthritis. She had spared him the news of her worsening condition in her letters. Whatever Lee might have felt at the moment, he never did reveal his feelings to anyone. Instead, from the first moment he discovered his crippled wife all he ever showed her was the patient attention he had shown his own dying mother.

Lee was forced to request temporary leave from the army to straighten out the mess in which his father-in-law had left his affairs. Now fifty-two, for the first time in his life he became a planter, finally straightening out the entangled Washington Custis estate.

JOHN BROWN RAIDS HARPER'S FERRY

One morning in October of 1859 a young cavalry lieutenant called on Lee at Arlington. Lee immediately recognized J. E. B. Stuart who had been a cadet at West Point when Lee was commandant. Lt. Stuart had come with an urgent message for Lee. The colonel was to accompany him immediately to the War Department. Something important had come up. There President Buchanan and Secretary of War Floyd informed Lee that Kansas border guerrillas under a man named "Smith" were heading a slave insurrection at Harper's Ferry, Virginia, and they had already seized the government arsenal there. "Slave insurrection" was enough to send a chill up any Southerner's spine.

Lee, Stuart, and a company of Marines under Lt. Israel Greene sped from Washington. Arriving at Harper's Ferry at dusk, to their relief they found no slave uprising as feared, and the band of abolitionist raiders had holed up in a locomotive roundhouse, using it as a fortress. Next morning, in a parley with the cooped-up insurrectionists, Jeb Stuart recognized their bearded leader peering out of the partly open doors as not "Smith," but John Brown. At a given signal the Marines rushed the engine house and battered in the doors. Lt. Greene lunged at John Brown with his dress sword. But it bent. So he beat Brown unconscious with the hilt. The fighting was suddenly over, and Lee took John Brown prisoner together with the four of his band left alive and unwounded.

Lewis Washington, one of John Brown's prisoner-hostages leaves us a vivid account of the action inside the roundhouse. "Brown was the coolest and bravest man I ever saw in defying danger and death," he reported. "With one son dead by his side, and another shot through, he felt the pulse of his dying son with one hand and held his rifle with the other and commanded his men with the utmost composure, encouraging them to be firm and sell their lives as dearly as they could."

John Brown was hanged on Dec. 2, 1859. Although Lee had been able to put down the "slave insurrection" in less than an hour, the very fact that it had been led by John Brown, a bible-quoting white man, made him frighteningly aware of the gathering storm.

THE AGONIZING DECISION

When Lee left to rejoin his regiment in Texas in February of 1860, more and more frequent talk of secession could be heard everywhere, prompting him to write in a letter, "I am not pleased with the course of the 'cotton states,' as they term themselves. . . ."

It was a troubled Lee stationed at a frontier post near San Antonio in 1861, when he wrote to one of his sons that he could conceive of no greater calamity than the dissolution of the Union which the Lee family and close friends of the family had helped bring into being. "Secession," he wrote, "is nothing but revolution." (Secession, at this time, was also termed treason by leading Virginia statesmen.) Yet, Lee continued, "a Union that can only be maintained by swords and bayonets, and in which strife and civil war are to take the place of brotherly love and kindness, has no charm for me. I shall mourn for my country and for the welfare and progress of mankind. If the Union is dissolved, and the government disrupted, I shall return to my native state and share the miseries of my people, and, save in her defense, will draw my sword no more."

Now fifty-four, and beginning to turn grey, with a majestic look to his growing maturity, Lee was riding to take command of the regiment at Fort Mason a hundred miles north of San Antonio, when the bombshell burst. News of the secession of the state of South Carolina had just reached Texas. General Beauregard had demanded the surrender of Fort Sumter in Charleston harbor on Apr. 11, 1861. Maj. Robert Anderson, United States Army, refused and Beauregard ordered the bombardment to commence. Maj. Anderson finally surrendered the fort on Apr. 14, and next day President Lincoln called up 75,000 militia by states.

Less than three weeks after South Carolina seceded, other states followed her lead, and from Jan, 9 to 26, 1861 Mississippi, Florida, Alabama, Georgia, and Louisiana also seceded. Then on Feb. 1 the Texas Convention overrode Sam Huston and Texas became the seventh state to secede. On Feb. 4 Virginia sent a commission to Washington to try and act as emissaries for a peaceful settlement, and on Feb. 13 Lee received orders relieving him of duty and instructing him to report to Washington. Talk was that Gen. Winfield Scott was preparing to launch an invasion of the South to put down the rebellion. Lee was beginning to agonize over the decision he might soon have to make, telling one of his younger officers that he devoutly hoped some agreement could be reached to avert a decision by arms. But as for himself, he added ruefully, he had no choice. If events forced Virginia to secede too, he would offer his state his services. Under no condition would he lift his sword against "Virginia's sons." As Lee spoke of this awful possibility, his usual control broke and he turned away from his young subordinate to hide his emotions.

Encountering another Unionist friend, Charles Anderson, brother of the Maj. Robert Anderson who had just surrendered Fort Sumter, Lee said, "I still think . . . that my loyalty to Virginia ought to take precedence over what is due the Federal government. And I shall so report myself in Washington. If Virginia stands by the old Union, so will I. But if she secedes (although I do not believe in secession as a constitutional right, nor is there sufficient cause for revolution), then I will still follow my native state with my sword and if need be with my life. I know you think and feel very differently, but I can't help it. These are my principles and I must follow them."

A few days after Lee had returned home to Arlington without a command, still clinging to the hope that reason would prevail, he read the newspaper account of Lincoln's inaugural address. "We are not enemies, but friends. . . .," Lincoln addressed the South. "Though passion may be strained, it must not break the bonds of affection. The mystic chords of memory, stretching from every battlefield and patriot grave to every living heart and hearthstone . . . will yet swell the chorus of the Union. When again touched, as surely they will be, by the better angels of our nature . . . the government will not assail you. You can have no conflict without yourselves being the aggressors."

Lincoln also promised that he had no intention of interfering with slavery wherever it existed, adding, "I believe I have no right to do so." Stating that he still considered the Union unbroken, Lincoln continued, "I shall take care, as the Constitution itself expressly enjoins upon me, that the laws of the Union be faithfully executed in all states. . . . In doing this there needs to be no bloodshed or violence; and there shall be none unless it be forced upon the national authority."

Then Lincoln came to the point, stating, "The power confided to me will be used to hold, occupy, and possess the property and places belonging to the government and to collect the duties and imposts; beyond what may be necessary for these objects, there will be no invasion—no using of force against or among people anywhere."

Lee knew what was coming. As tension mounted, in March General-in-Chief of the Army Scott appointed Lee a full colonel to assume command of the First U.S. Cavalry, and President Lincoln quickly signed Lee's commission. Earlier Scott had held an interview with his fellow-Virginian Lee, but neither man ever revealed the gist of the conversation. Only Mrs. Lee could provide the possible answer when she wrote, "My husband was summoned to Washington where every motive and argument was used to induce him to accept the command of the army destined to invade the South."

On Apr. 18 Lee was again called to Washington to meet with old Francis P. Blair, a power in Washington politics for thirty years. Blair came right to the point. He was authorized by the President to offer Lee command of the new army then being raised. As he recalled later, Lee told Mr. Blair, "Though opposed to secession and deprecating war, I could take no part in invasion of the Southern states." Thanking Mr. Blair for his consideration, Lee left the Blair House across Pennsylvania Avenue from the White House and proceeded for the last time to Gen. Scott's office in the War Department. When he reported his conversation with Blair, Scott blurted out, "Lee, you have made the greatest mistake of your life." Then, as an afterthought, he added, "But I feared it would be so." Sadly Scott told Lee that under the circumstances he thought he ought to resign his commission in the United States Army.

The next day there was no question about it. President Lincoln included Virginia among the states called upon to furnish troops for an invasion of the Southern states then in rebellion. Now the Virginia Convention, which had previously voted two-to-one against secession, turned right around and voted two-to-one against furnishing troops and to secede.

Lee now found himself in the midst of an agonizing dilemma. He had to make a choice. On the one hand, there was the country he had served so faithfully as a soldier for thirty-six years. On the other, his love of Virginia, the state to which he owed his very birth and heritage. Lee spent the rest of the day upstairs in his room. Downstairs in her wheelchair his wife could hear him pacing back and forth on the floor above. Finally, after midnight he came downstairs and handed her the letter he had written to Scott:

"General:

"Since my interview with you on the 18th inst. I have felt that I ought not longer retain my commission in the army. I therefore tender my resignation, which I request you will recommend for acceptance.

"It would have been presented at once, but for the struggle it has cost me to separate myself from a service to which I had devoted all the best years of my life and all the ability I possess.

"During the whole of that time, more than thirty-six years, I have experienced nothing but kindness from my superiors, and a most cordial friendship from my companions. To no one, General, have I been as much indebted as to yourself for uniform kindness and consideration, and it has always been my ardent desire to meet your approbation.

"I shall carry with me to the grave the most grateful recollections of your kind consideration and your name and fame will always be dear to me. Save in defense of my Native State, I never desire again to draw my sword.

"Be pleased to accept my most earnest wishes for the continuance of your happiness and prosperity and believe me

Most truly yours,

R. E. Lee"

After Lee made his agonizing and fateful decision, he explained his action in a letter to his sister in Baltimore, writing, "The whole South is in a state of revolution, into which Virginia, after a long struggle, has been drawn; and though I recognize no necessity with this state of things, and would have forborne and pleaded to the end for a redress of grievances, real or supposed, yet in my own person I had to meet the question whether I should take part against my native state. With all my devotion to the Union and a feeling of loyalty and duty as an American citizen, I have not been able to make up my mind to raise my hand against my relatives, my children, and my home. I have therefore resigned my commission in the army. . . ."

Now fifty-four, Lee presented a strikingly handsome figure of a man. He stood ramrod-straight, five feet ten inches tall. Powerfully but compactly built, he weighed only 170 pounds. His hair and full moustache were still dark, though showing signs of grey. (But by 1863 he would be snow-white.) He cast an aura of dignity about him that commanded both attention and respect. A private who once fought under him said that Lee "looked like some good boy's grandpa," adding, "His whole makeup of form and person, looks and manner, had a gentle and soothing magnetism about it. I fell in love with the old gentleman."

THE CONFEDERATE

Two days after he submitted his resignation Lee was called to Richmond by Governor John Letcher. When the Southern states first began to secede, Letcher had advocated a convention to discuss measures for preventing secession. When that failed, he tried to promote the idea of a Peace Commission led by former President Tyler. But when Lincoln called on Virginia for volunteers to invade sister Southern states, Letcher immediately wired Lincoln, "You have chosen to inaugurate civil war."

Gov. Letcher got right down to business, informing Lee that he had been recommended to command Virginia's military and naval forces with the rank of major general. Lee accepted, stating, "Mr. President and Gentlemen of the Convention: Profoundly impressed by the solemnity of the occasion, for which I must say I was not prepared, I accept the position assigned me by your partiality. I would have much preferred had your choice fallen on an abler man. Trusting in Almighty God, and approving conscience, and the aid of my fellow citizens, I devote myself to the service of my native state in whose behalf will I ever draw my sword."

In a letter to his wife Lee wrote, "War is inevitable and there is no telling when it will burst around you. . . . You have to move and make arrangements to go to some point of safety which you must select. The Mount Vernon plate and pictures ought to be secured. Keep quiet while you remain and in your preparations. . . . God keep and preserve you and have mercy on all our people."

There were no government arsenals as in the Old Army now to furnish arms. The only rifle-producing facility in the Confederacy was at Harper's Ferry and the only cannon-producing works at Norfolk. Accordingly, Gov. Letcher directed Lee to order Col. Thomas J. Jackson to assume command at Harper's Ferry. At the time, Jackson was an instructor at VMI where he was known as "Fool Tom" and the "crazy" one for his weird diets, strange practices, and eccentricities. But Jackson brought much-needed discipline to the outpost training camp at Harper's Ferry and immediately showed that he understood Lee's intentions. Lee did not want to invite an enemy attack until his poorly armed and clothed green troops could be molded into soldiers. The other professional army officers coming home did not want to be hurried into action any more than Lee. While the professional soldiers who knew war understood Lee's purposes, civilians did not. One show of force by the South, they figured, and the Yankees would be sent scurrying home and the war would be over in a single engagement. A representative of the slave interests even had the gall to declare that Lee was not in sympathy with the Confederate cause when Lee dismissed his demand for instant action.

Lee wrote his wife, "I agree with you in thinking that the inflammatory articles in the papers do us much harm. I object particularly to those in the Southern papers, as I wish them to take a firm, dignified course free of bravado and boasting. The times are indeed calamitous. . . ."

When Virginia's armed forces were absorbed by the Confederacy, Lee thought he would be given a field command. But President Davis had other ideas. "I do not know what my position will be," Lee wrote his wife on June 9. "I should like to retire to private life so that I could be with you and the children. But if I can be of service to the state or our cause, I must continue." Although Lee was appointed a full general in the Confederate army on June 14, 1861, a full year was to pass before he would take command of any large-scale military operations.

Lee had known President Jefferson Davis since their days together as cadets at West Point, but never intimately. With his feeling of superiority—more, infallibility—and his insensitivity to the feelings of others, the Confederate President was a very difficult person to get along with. He suffered from neuralgic facial spasms and upset stomach and he had lost one eye, probably due to glaucoma, while his remaining eye gave him constant pain. Perhaps these physical ailments made the egotistical, thin-skinned man even more short-tempered and sharp-tongued. To disagree with Davis in anything, no matter how trivial, was to make a lifelong enemy. Maybe his very absence of political adroitness was what drew Lee to the man, for Lee always had a basic distrust of politicians. He trusted Davis and believed that no man ever gave himself more completely to a cause. It was Lee's unusual gift for getting along with people and his excellent judgment of character that enabled him to bring out the best in Davis and avoid conflict.

Up to now it had been largely a war in name only. But this situation was soon to change. On July 21, 1861 Brig. Gen. Irvin McDowell attacked Beauregard's forces at Bull Run. The Confederates routed the Federals. It was in this battle that Jackson got his immortal nickname when someone shouted in the thick of it, "Look! There is Jackson standing like a *stone wall!*"

In this first test of strength had not the Southern zealots proved their point? At the first clash the Yankees had fled the field in panic. Soldiers who arrived in Manassas after the battle felt ashamed to go home without ever firing a shot in this quick war, now "won." The attempt at quick suppression of the rebellious Southern states was over, to be sure, but as Lee knew all too well, a long, all-out war had just begun. On July 26 the U. S. Congress authorized 500,000 men for the U. S. Army.

After the Confederate victory at Bull Run Lee wrote his wife to tell her how bad he felt about not being able to be in the thick of it. "But the President thought it more important I should be there," he wrote. "I could not have done as well as has been done, but I could have helped and taken part in the struggle for my home and neighborhood. So the work is done, I care not by whom it is done."

WESTERN VIRGINIA IS LOST

Between July 1861 and June 1862 President Davis let a lull fall over the Confederacy. On July 28 Lee was sent to the western mountains to try and salvage a hopeless command situation there.

Coordinating three prima donnas—Loring, Wise, and Floyd——without any authority over them, supervising the scattered forces then defending western Virginia, and coordinating the movements of small armies under the command of these three egotistical and jealous generals was an impossible task.

About now, Lee was growing accustomed to a new horse he had purchased in the western mountains which he named "Traveller." A strongly built five-year-old, standing sixteen hands, Traveller was, as Lee described him, "Confederate grey," with black points and small head. Horse and rider immediately took to each other and soon the big grey became Lee's favorite mount. Foaled near Blue Sulphur in 1857, Traveller served as Lee's principal mount all during and after the war. (He outlived Lee.) The horse had amazing speed and endurance, frequently tiring out the horses of Lee's staff. With remarkable stamina, only twice did he become frightened by shells bursting around him, once rearing in time to save Lee's life, as a cannonball passed harmlessly under his girth, scraping the soles of Lee's boots.

In the dismal camp in the mountains of western Virginia Lee stopped shaving altogether. His full beard now grew out solid grey. Even though he was not their commander, the men in the ranks affectionately referred to Lee as "Uncle Robert," "Mr. Robert," or plain "Marse Robert," as it came out slurred in their careless Southern drawl.

Early in September Floyd wrote Lee that the Union army threatened to lay waste to the countryside. On Sept. 7 Lee replied, "I cannot believe that the enemy will carry out their threat of burning and laying waste to the countryside. It is intended to intimidate. The sentiment in America will not tolerate it."—Lee would live to eat these words!

In early October Lee toyed with the idea of trying to mount an offensive into western Virginia, but everything worked against it. His failure to advance anything of consequence raised a public clamor. In the end Lee was able to do little more than save the Confederate units there from complete annihilation at the hands of larger, more effective Federal armies. The western counties were soon lost to the enemy and Lee returned to Richmond as the scapegoat for the reverses. Some now began to refer to Virginia's first soldier as "Granny."

In March of 1862 Davis named Lee his chief military adviser and before long the President showed his confidence in Lee by putting him in charge of the conduct of the military operations of the armies of the Confederacy. Lee showed that he was not pleased by the weak efforts of many Southerners when he wrote his daughter, "Our people have not been earnest enough, have thought too much of themselves and their ease, and instead of turning out to a man, have been content to nurse themselves and their dimes and leave the protection of themselves and families to others. To satisfy their consciences they have been clamorous in criticizing what others have done and endeavored to prove that they ought to do nothing. This is not the way to accomplish our independence."

'BUT RICHMOND MUST BE DEFENDED!'

Lee was opposed to President Davis' scheme of static defense and Johnston's plan to implement it. Where Davis needed to provide against all possible contingencies, Lee had never forgotten the lesson of Gen. Winfield Scott's exploiting battlefield opportunities. Lee's thinking leaned toward engaging the enemy as far from the capital as possible. And he would never choose to concentrate, as Johnston planned, for a purely defensive stand. A good attack, Lee believed, was the best defense.

Lee's brilliance as a military strategist began to emerge that spring. Gen. George B. McClellan was now amassing the mightiest military force ever to set foot on American soil. By the end of March McClellan's superbly equipped Army of the Potomac, 110,000 strong, was embarked on river boats, floated down the Potomac, and landed by sea near old Point Comfort or Fort Monroe on the York Peninsula just seventy miles from Richmond. Johnston's first reaction was to fall back in the face of superior numbers, but President Davis ordered him, "Yorktown must be defended!" And McClellan wasted a month on siege operations at Yorktown against only 16,000 Confederate defenders.

Lee realized the Confederates could never field the huge number of troops McClellan had. Yet a serious blow in another sector against the North might cripple McClellan's plans. Now after almost a year as a desk general, Lee would have the chance of testing his theory of "disrupting the enemy's prearrangements." His immediate objective was to fend off McDowell's threat from Fredericksburg to the north. At the same time, unbeknownst to either Davis or Johnston, he secretly planned to launch smashing surprise diversionary attacks in the Shenandoah Valley led by Stonewall Jackson. The Valley Campaign of 1862 would prove to be one of the most brilliant moves in military history.

On May 4 Johnston secretly moved his troops out of Yorktown. McClellan's advance troops clashed with Longstreet's rear guard at Williamsburg May 5. And for the next three weeks he and "Little Mac" played cat-and-mouse while Stonewall Jackson moved up the Shenandoah Valley, diverting U. S. troops and executing a series of swift marches and smashing victories. Surprising the Federal armies and sending them reeling in retreat, Jackson now posed a threat to Washington.

Lee's strategic masterpiece had worked to perfection. A worried Union Secretary Stanton ordered McDowell's corps back to defend Washington. Jackson and his little army then hurried south to join Lee and Johnston before Richmond, where by the end of May McClellan was finally closing in.

President Davis so was convinced that Richmond was doomed, that he had already sent his family south to Raleigh. When Lee was called to a meeting to discuss the next line of defense after Richmond was abandoned, he stared at the President and the other silent men in disbelief. No one had ever heard Lee speak except in his soft mild bass. Now he roared in a voice shaking with emotion, "But Richmond *must* be defended!"

On June 1 Johnston launched a poorly organized attack against McClellan's two corps on the south side of the Chickahominy. In the indecisive Battle of Fair Oaks or Seven Pines seven miles east of Richmond, Johnston was critically wounded. But he did succeed in stopping McClellan's advance. Davis put Lee in command of the army. Now the old soldier would attempt something he had never done before in his thirty-seven years as an officer—command troops in combat.

COMMANDER WITHOUT COMBAT EXPERIENCE

Lee knew he was being received with less than complete enthusiasm as the new army commander. Even Jeb Stuart wrote his wife that he was disappointed in the selection of Lee. Yet in three weeks time Lee organized a retreating hodgepodge force of Confederate troops on the outskirts of Richmond into the legendary Army of Northern Virginia. As soon as he took command, Lee rode about the lines so his men could become familiar with the commanding general, the composed grey figure on his composed grey horse. When at first his men were opposed to digging in, Lee wrote Davis, "Our troops, officers, community, and press ridicule and resist it. It is the very means by which McClellan has and is advancing. Why should we leave to him the whole advantage of labor? Combined with valor, fortitude, and boldness, of which we have our fair proportion, it should lead us to success. What carried the Roman soldiers into all countries but this happy combination? . . . There is nothing so military as labor and nothing so important to any army as to save the lives of its soldiers."

Lee had no intention of waiting for McClellan to complete his preparations for the siege of Richmond. Instead, he would completely "disrupt the enemy's prearrangements," and not merely lift the siege of Richmond, but "drive our enemies back to their homes," and "change the character of the war."

As a master of the unexpected and an unwavering proponent of maximum concentration of force against isolated segments of the enemy army, Lee promptly made plans for a massive counterattack. Even the generals Lee had selected to lead the offensive were kept in the dark until they were called to his headquarters on June 23. Lee had already weeded out those commanders with a negative or defeatist attitude. To one officer attempting to demonstrate to Lee with paper and pencil how McClellan's advance could not be stopped, Lee suddenly interrupted, "Stop! If you go on ciphering, we are whipped beforehand!" Earlier Lee had confided to his staff, "If we leave this line because they can shell us, we shall have to leave the next for the same reason. And I don't see how we can stop this side of Richmond."

Lee started the Seven Days Battle at Mechanicsville on June 26. McClellan dropped back to Gaines Mill. In the confusion, everything was going wrong. Things were not going according to plan. Jackson, late in arriving, finally came trotting in at about five p.m. Facing the collapse of his first battle, Lee greeted him with a touch of sarcasm, "Ah, General," he said acidly, "I am very glad to see you. I had hoped to be with you before this." Jackson made no excuses, even though he had good ones. Then Lee added, "That fire is very heavy. Do you think your men can stand it?" "They can stand anything," Jackson snapped. "They can stand that."

The battle was hanging in the balance when Lee risked a decisive defeat in committing himself to win. It was very late in the day to mount an assault for a decision. But this is just what Lee ordered. When John Hood finally made his breakthrough at dusk, Lee knew he had won his first battle. About 8,000 Confederate dead and wounded lay in the field after the battle. But this was a battle Lee had to win regardless of cost.

PERFECT TRAP FAILS

In a series of tough battles in the Seven Days struggle McClellan was finally pushed back to the wharves of Berkeley Plantation where he began. After first routing McClellan, Lee set what he thought was the perfect trap at Glendale June 30. But it failed. Lee realized the tremendous opportunity of destroying the enemy army he had seen slip through his fingers, and the disappointment was more than he could hide. Longstreet observed, "The composure with which it was born indicated the grander elements of his character, and it drew those who knew his plans and purposes closer to him."

On the Fourth of July Lee made a personal reconnaissance to see if there was any way of getting at McClellan on the flat lands of Berkeley Plantation. Summing up his findings in a letter to President Davis, he wrote, "I fear he (McCellan) is too secure under cover of his boats to be driven from his position. I discover no intention of (his) either ascending or crossing the river at present. Reinforcements have joined him and his sick, wounded, and demoralized troops have been sent down the river."

Because the Peninsula victory was the first major victory for the Confederacy since Bull Run, halting a series of reverses in the west, a new surge of aggressive spirit swept through the South. Lee emerged overnight as the people's deliverer and hero and the most famous soldier in the world. His soldiers developed an almost mystical belief in him, although his army had suffered heavy losses, nearly one fourth of his total command.

Lee at Fredericksburg, December 13, 1862

Following the debacle of the Peninsular Campaign, Halleck became general-in-chief of the Federal forces and McClellan was succeeded by Maj. Gen. John Pope. Lee respected McClellan as a soldier. But this Pope was a different breed. Halleck decided to try the original plan for 1862, a frontal advance from Washington on Richmond. But Pope, who was to command the offensive in the field, had little military ability. His first act on taking command was to proclaim to the press, "My headquarters will be in the saddle." On reading this account, Lincoln said, "A better place for his hindquarters." Lee's officers made the obvious comments about where they thought Pope's brains were.

Pope became the first soldier in the struggle to declare war on civilians. According to his harsh orders, Union soldiers were to live off the people; all men within the Federal lines were to be arrested, and if they refused to take the oath of allegiance to the United States, they were to be driven out. Finally, Pope proclaimed that any person within the lines who wrote a letter to a Confederate soldier was to be considered a spy and become subject to the death penalty. Lee wrote to McClellan and Pope drew in his horns a little. But now something very ugly had come to the struggle. Gone were the high-principled restraints once stated by a colonel in McClellan's army from New York State. Northern soldiers, he had said, must remember that they and the Southerners were one people, and acts must be avoided that tended to widen the breech. Pope, however, introduced the feeling of hatred into the struggle.

SECOND BULL RUN

Lee was trying to figure out how to dispose of Pope, while containing McClellan, and at the same time keeping an eye on Burnside's force in transports off the coast of Fort Monroe. When Lee learned that Burnside had landed in Fredericksburg and had started west to join Pope, and that McClellan's army was leaving Berkeley Plantation, undoubtedly to join Pope, too, the race was on.

In mid-August Lee again decided on a plan as bold as it was brilliant. Against all military commandments, he was going to divide his numerically inferior army and send Jackson on a wide flanking movement around Pope's right to attack the Union base at Manassas Junction. He thus unfolded what was to become his basic offensive pattern throughout the war: a wide flanking movement by one segment of his army to divert attention, followed by smashing assaults on both front and flank of the enemy force facing him.

Lee removed a few units from the Richmond line as a feeler. Then he asked the President if he thought Richmond could be held if he took on Pope. Lee told Davis, "The whole army, I think, should be united here as soon as possible. I . . . will direct Gen. Smith to send on McLaw's, D. H. Hill's, and other available troops. Should you not agree with me in the propriety of this step, please countermand the order and let me know." Next day Lee pressed the point with the President. "I believe a portion of McClellan's army has now joined Pope," he wired. "Expedite the advance of our troops."

For a man of Davis' personality, the President's answer was one of the finest. "Generals Hill and McLaw, at North Anna (River), ordered to join you. The brigades of Ransome and Walker start from here this morning." Then Davis continued, "Confidence in you overcomes the view which would otherwise be taken of the exposed condition of Richmond, and the troops retained for the defense of the capital are surrendered to you on a renewed request."

On Aug. 26, when Lee received Davis' reply, he was already on his way. Without waiting for the reinforcements, he was advancing towards Washington where 150,000 Federal troops were concentrating. The same day, Jackson's "foot cavalry," marching fifty-four miles in a day and a half, were on Pope's rear, between him and Washington, digging into Pope's vast stores at Manassas Junction at the old Bull Run battlefield.

Lee never ordered—he suggested. As Longstreet said later, his instructions for the Second Battle of Bull Run were, "General Lee is inclined to engage as soon as practicable, but did not so order."

Pope was badly defeated in the Second Battle of Bull Run and Manassas Aug. 29 and 30, 1862, and his army fled in panic back to Washington. The irresistible combination of Lee's audacious strategy and Jackson's perfect tactics had undone the Union's gains of an entire year in the Virginia theater of war.

As the firing died off at Bull Run, Lee halted Traveller a few feet from one of his smoking guns. A ragged, powder-blackened young gunner was brought to him by one of his staff officers. Lee was accustomed to privates addressing him directly, and when his staff officer said, "General, here is someone who wants to speak to you," Lee said to the weary soldier, "Well, my man, what can I do for you?" "Why, General, don't you know me?" came the startled young voice. Lee and his son Rob had a good laugh over the incident.

FIRST PUSH INTO THE NORTH

Since the Civil War many historians have been puzzled over Lee's actions following Second Manassas. After the war, when Lee was asked why he had crossed the Potomac and gone into Maryland, he replied to feed his army. This was partly true. But there was much more to it. The moment was now opportune, he reasoned, to carry the war into the North. An invasion of Northern territory might produce a decisive, war-ending victory. If not, it might prompt recognition from England and France as well as secure Maryland for the Confederacy. In any event, his army could still obtain much-needed supplies in the North. The plan also conformed to Lee's offensive-defensive strategy of confounding his opponents by feints and actual movements against the North. But most of all, this was the period of balance when it seemed possible to achieve peace and Southern independence. Tipping the balance on the other side, however, word was now out that Lincoln had prepared his Emancipation Proclamation in recognition of the need for a popular crusade in support of the war.

On Sept. 4 Lee's army of 50,000 splashed across the Potomac into Maryland. On Sept. 8 Lee wrote Davis from Frederick:

"The present posture of affairs, in my opinion, places it in the power of the Government of the Confederate States to propose with propriety to that of the United States recognition of our independence.

"For more than a year both sections of the country have been devastated by hostilities which have brought sorrow and suffering upon thousands of homes, without advancing the objectives which our enemies have proposed to themselves in beginning the contest.

"Such a proposition, coming from us at this time, could in no way be regarded as a suing for peace, but being made when it is now in our power to inflict injury upon our adversary, would show conclusively to the world that our sole object is the establishment of our independence and the attainment of an honorable peace. The rejection of this offer would prove to the country that the responsibility for the continuance of the war does not rest upon us, but that the party in power in the United States elects to prosecute it for a purpose of their own. The proposal of peace would enable the people of the United States to determine at their coming elections whether they favor those who favor a prolongation of the war or those who wish to bring it to a termination, which can but be productive of good to both parties without affecting the honor of either."

The General discusses the situation with Jefferson Davis and the Cabinet.

WAR IS TERRIBLE

One morning in October a staff officer entered Lee's tent to find the old soldier overcome with grief, tears streaming down his cheeks, staring at an open letter he held in his hand. Lee's twenty-three-year-old daughter Annie had died after a brief illness. But this was no time for mourning. McClellan had started south on the east side of the Blue Ridge, and on Oct. 28 Lee broke camp and his army of ragged veterans was on the march again. Suddenly, McClellan's army turned toward Fredericksburg. Although Lee did not know it at the time, McClellan had been relieved of command for good.

Early in December the new commander of the Army of the Potomac, Gen. Ambrose E. Burnside, pushed toward Richmond. The weather was very cold, and it was hard on Lee to see his men shivering in their ragged clothes and the bloody tracks their bare feet left in the snow. When Burnside crossed the Rappahannock, Lee, with Longstreet and Jackson and 75,000 men, took his stand in an almost impregnable position on wooded Marye's Heights above Fredericksburg and on Dec. 13 met an attack by Burnside's army of 113,000 in what was probably the most useless slaughter of the Civil War. Refusing to make flanking attacks through the forest, Burnside insanely ordered frontal attacks across open ground completely swept by Confederate artillery fire. Six times the Union infantry were thrown back, leaving thousands of killed and wounded heaped in piles on the battlefield. It was during the carnage at Fredericksburg that Lee made his famous observation, "It is well this (the war) is so terrible, else we should grow too fond of it." Lee consented to a brief truce to bury the dead and help the wounded.

The bitter cold and lack of food were taking their toll. "I am willing to starve myself, but can not bear my men and horses to be pinched," Lee wrote. Then to his son Curtis his wrote, "Men and animals have suffered much from scarcity of food, and I fear they are destined to more. I am doubtful whether I will be able to retain my position and may at last be obliged to yield to a greater force than that under command of General Hooker." With hunger everywhere around him, Lee wrote, "We shall lose the moral advantages we had gained and our men may become discouraged." At headquarters, too, Lee's staff complained of the near-starvation diet Lee insisted on sharing with his men.

Meanwhile, in other theaters of the war, Charleston was being threatened in the east and the Confederates faced another enemy offensive in the west. Joe Johnston, now recovered from his wounds, had gone west as department commander. On Apr. 9 Lee wrote, "The readiest method of relieving the pressure on Gen. Johnston and Gen. Beauregard at Charleston would be for the army to cross into Maryland."

THE BLOODY BATTLE OF ANTIETAM

Now we come to one of those strange and unpredictable quirks in the fortunes of war. When Lee's army left Frederick, Maryland, the three most important cigars in history were left behind by some unidentified staff officer wrapped in an extra copy of an order showing the complete disposition of Lee's divided army. When the Federal troops reached Frederick, the prize trophy was found. As a result, two armies that were gathering around a town of no particular strategic importance to either (Sharpsburg) on the banks of Antietam Creek began one of the bloodiest one-day engagements of the Civil War. Of the Union's 77,000 engaged, 13,000 fell. Of the Confederates' 50,000 engaged, another 13,000 joined the mass of dead and wounded on the battlefield. Lee never explained why he made a stand where he was. Perhaps he was unwilling to abandon his high hopes and dreams for the campaign and return to Virginia after scarcely more than a week on Maryland soil.

Lee's withdrawal from Northern territory provided Lincoln with the favorable conditions and timing for his political masterstroke of the war. Shrewdly using the bloody Battle of Antietam as the basis for issuing his famous Emancipation Proclamation, Lincoln thus elevated the war to a struggle for human freedom as well as preservation of the Union. On Sept. 22, 1862, three days after Lee was back in Virginia, Lincoln declared that on Jan. 1, 1863 all slaves in the territory then in rebellion would be declared free. In one sense, the Proclamation gave the Unionists the illusion that their fight to free the slaves was a moral crusade. In another sense, it backfired. The South's leaders and newspapers regarded the humanistic trappings as deceit, stigmatizing all Southerners as fighting to preserve chattel slavery. As the Richmond *Examiner* wrote, "A candid world" (would interpret the Proclamation) "an act of malice toward the master rather than one of mercy for the slave." The effects of the Emancipation were soon seen in a new harshness in prosecuting the war and a new hardening of Southern resolve and determination to resist and be free of the North.

'CAST IN A GRANDER MOLD'

In the six weeks of rest during late September and October Lee's army of ragamuffins received packages from home containing clothes left behind from civilian days. But no shoes. Many of the men made sandles out of tanned hides. But in the end many were still walking barefoot.

Respect, not sentries, was the only barrier to Lee's tent. A distinguished British visitor, Colonel, later Viscount, Wolseley, reported, "While all honor him, those with whom he is the most intimate feel the affection for him of sons to a father." "I have met many of the great men of my time," said Wolseley, "but Lee alone impressed me with the feeling I was in the presence of a man who was cast in a grander mold, and made of different and finer metal than all other men." Lee's hair and beard were nearly white now, he noted. "But his dark brown eyes shine with all the brightness of youth, and beamed with the most pleasing expression. Indeed, his whole face is kindly and benevolent in the highest degree. In manner, though sufficiently conversable, he is slightly reserved; but he is a person that, wherever seen, whether in a castle or a hovel, alone or in a crowd, must at once attract attention as being a splendid specimen of an English gentleman, with one of the most rarely handsome faces I ever saw."

JACKSON KILLED AT CHANCELLORSVILLE

Near the end of April 1863 Lee was still facing the Union army along the Rappahannock line. Maj. Gen. Joseph E. Hooker had succeeded Burnside. On Apr. 29 Lee was awakened to learn that Federal troops were crossing the river. Against the consensus of his other commanders, Lee was certain that the United States force on the plain below Fredericksburg was just a threat and the movement around Chancellorsville was Hooker's main effort.

Advancing southward in two wings, each of which was larger than Lee's 60,000-man army, Hooker's plan was to destroy the Army of Northern Virginia with superior manpower in a powerful two-pronged attack. Now came Lee's finest hour as a military strategist. While Hooker had caught him in the jaws of his pincers, Lee immediately perceived that Hooker's army was also separated with Confederate troops in between. Hooker had also made the mistake of putting his army into the dense jungle-like country called The Wilderness.

Lee reacted with moves as dangerous as they were brilliant. Leaving a third of his army to confront the Union force at Fredericksburg, Lee hurried the rest of his army west. He further divided his tiny army by sending Jackson's corps of 32,000 on a 14-mile arc around Hooker's vulnerable right flank. Then Lee struck Hooker's isolated wing from two directions. In the ensuing Battle of

Chancellorsville May 1-4, 1863 Lee again sent a larger Federal force reeling in defeat.

But the Confederate victory at Chancellorsville was even costlier than the 17,197 Union casualties, 13,000 Confederate. Jackson and his staff were returning to their own lines after staking out the Union dispositions. Mistaking them for the enemy, a Confederate regiment swept Jackson's party with a deadly volley. Jackson caught two bullets in the left arm near the shoulder, crushing the main artery and his arm had to be amputated. Lee winced with a moan when he heard that Jackson had been wounded and tears sprang into his eyes. "Ah, Captain," he said to one of his staff, "any victory is dearly bought which deprives us of the services of General Jackson, even for a short time." Lee wrestled in prayer all night for Jackson's life, but Stonewall kept sinking and he lapsed into a coma. Suddenly Jackson cried out, "Order A. P. Hill to prepare for action. Pass the infantry to the front. Tell Major Hawks. . . ." His words faded off and once again he fell back into a coma. Late in the afternoon, right before he gave up the ghost, Jackson said in a low voice, "Let us cross over the river and rest in the shade under the trees." Then the intrepid Stonewall Jackson sank into death—in deathless fame.

When Hooker's troops fell back and Lee rode forward to meet Stuart at Chancellorsville, his troops spotted the unshakeable grey figure on his steady grey horse. "The sight of their leader served as a signal for one of those uncontrollable outbursts of enthusiasm which no one can appreciate who has not witnessed them," a staff officer reported. "The fierce soldiers, with their faces blackened from smoke of battle, the wounded crawling with feeble limbs from the devouring flames, all seemed possessed of a common impulse. One long, unbroken cheer rose high above the roar of battle."

'BOTH SIDES GOT THE WORST OF IT AT GETTYSBURG'

All of Lee's tactical successes thus far, however, had succeeded in producing no more than a stalemate on the Virginia front, while Federal forces won important victories in other parts of the Confederacy. If he again invaded the North, Lee figured, perhaps it might force Gen. Grant to relinquish his stranglehold on Vicksburg.

On June 1 Lee's 76,224 veterans and 272 guns again crossed the Potomac and within a short time were well on their way through

Maryland. Staking everything on one bold thrust, Lee planned to head northward into Pennsylvania where he could simultaneously threaten Harrisburg, Baltimore, and Washington. In this second invasion of the North, however, everything seemed to go against him. Jackson was no longer with him. And Federal cavalry captured Confederate dispatches announcing Lee's Northern plan. The Army of the Potomac, with 115,256 men (about 90,000 effective) and 362 guns followed in close pursuit. On Sunday June 21 Lee found himself in enemy territory without his cavalry. He never dreamed for a moment then that Jeb Stuart was off on one of his stunt rides and was cut off from his own army.

Outside Chambersburg, Pennsylvania, a local woman came to Lee's tent to appeal to him for food for families facing hunger after the Confederates had collected their cattle, hogs, flour, and molasses. Impressed by the strength and sadness in Lee's face, the woman impulsively asked him for his autograph. "Do you want the autograph of a Rebel?" he asked. "General Lee," she responded, "I am a true Union woman. Yet I ask for bread and your autograph." Writing "R. E. Lee" on a slip of paper, Lee handed it to the woman and remarked, "My only desire is that they will let me go home and eat my own bread in peace." Then Lee ordered his army, "The commanding general considers that no greater disgrace could befall the army, and throughout our whole people, than the perpetration of the barbarous outrages on the unarmed and the defenseless, and the wanton destruction of private property that have marked the course of the enemy in our own country. . . . It must be remembered that we make war only upon armed men and that we can not take vengeance for the wrongs our people have suffered without . . . offending against Him to whom vengeance belongeth, without whose favor and support our efforts must all prove in vain. . . ."

On June 29, Lee, without his cavalry, still had no clear idea of where his enemy was. Concentrating on the eastern slope of South Mountain near Cashtown, in a strong defensive position, Lee awaited attack. Lee did not know it yet, but on June 28 Lincoln had given Maj. Gen. George G. Meade top command of the Union army. Meade, too, intended to take a defensive position and let Lee attack him.

Desperate for information, Lee was told by a spy that two Federal corps were close to the mountains and knew where his army was. Also, Hooker had been replaced by Meade. This was sobering news—on both counts. George Gordon Meade, a friend from the Old Army, was no Hooker, Pope, or Burnside. He was the type of general, Lee said, who would make no blunder. "And if I make one," he added, "he will make haste to take advantage of it." Pacing restlessly outside his tent, when he was approached by one of his staff Lee immediately assumed his usual cheerful and composed manner. "The enemy is a long time in finding us," he said humorously. "If he does not succeed soon, we will go and search for him."

On June 30 a unit of A. P. Hill's corps covering Lee's concentration headed toward Gettysburg in search of shoes. Buford's First U. S. Cavalry held them up initially two miles outside town, but was pushed back on July 1. And the great three-day battle had begun, a chance contact placing the struggle where neither Lee nor Meade had wanted it. Ewell then forced the U. S. Army back to Cemetery Hill; Maj. Gen. Reynolds, U.S.A., was killed. The Federal forces then took Culp's Hill, extending the line to Round Top. Lee's attacks were checked the next day, and on July 3 Maj. Gen. George E. Pickett, Maj. Gen. Isaac Trimble, and Brig. Gen. James J. Pettigrew, with 12,400 men, made their disastrous charge against the Federal center but were repulsed. His expression unchanging, Lee mounted Traveller and rode down from his command post to take the survivors of the costly charge back under his wing. "Don't be discouraged," he kept saying as he rode among the dazed survivors, many of them wounded. "It was all my fault this time. . . . All good men must hold together now."

Only about a third of Pickett's men made it out. Pickett rode up and cried out hysterically that his division was destroyed. "Come, General Pickett," Lee said softly. "This has been my fight, and upon my shoulders rests the blame. The men and officers of your command have written the name of Virginia today as high as it has ever been written before."

Wearily dismounting at his headquarters tent after dark, Lee threw his arm across the saddle and rested on it. "The moon shown full upon his massive features and revealed an expression of sadness that I had never before seen upon his face," a staff member reported. "General, this has been a hard day for you," the staff officer said to comfort him in his anguish. Lee, raising his head, and making no effort to hide his grief, replied, "Yes, yes, it has been a sad, sad day for us." Then, choking with emotion, he said, "I never saw troops behave more magnificently than Pickett's division of Virginia did in that grand charge upon the enemy. And if they had been supported as they should have been, but for some reason not explained to me were not, we would have held the position and the day would have been ours." Then in absolute anguish Lee moaned, "Too bad! Too bad! Oh, too bad!" Finally himself again, Lee straightened up and said, "We must now return to Virginia."

As one soldier in a North Carolina regiment summed up the awful slaughter, "Both sides got the worst of it at Gettysburg." Still Lee's army was not wrecked. Only three brigades of thirty-seven on the field were hurt beyond immediate repair. Meade did not counterattack, and after waiting a day Lee withdrew and began his slow and sad retreat back to Virginia.

'I AM ALONE TO BLAME'

"No blame can be attached to the army for its failure to accomplish what was projected by me," Lee wrote Davis, "nor should it be censured for the unreasonable expectation of the public. I am alone to blame."

On July 4, the day after Lee's repulse at Gettysburg, the second bit of bad news broke. Vicksburg had been surrendered to Grant. Depression spread throughout the Confederacy.

Lee made more comments about the Battle of Gettysburg than he did about any other battle of the war. The strongest feeling he expressed was his grief over the appalling number of casualties, writing, "The loss of our gallant officers and men throughout the army causes me to weep tears of blood and to wish that I could never hear the sound of a gun again. My only consolation is that they are the happier, and we that are left are to be pitied."

After reading a detailed criticism in the Charleston *Mercury*, he wrote, "I much regret its general censure on the operations of the army, and is calculated to do us no good either at home or abroad. But I am prepared for similar criticisms, and so far as I am concerned the remarks fall harmless. . . . To take notice of such attacks would, I think, do more harm than good, and would be just what is desired. . . . No blame can be attached to the army for its failure to accomplish what was projected by me, nor should it be censured for the unreasonable expectation of the public. I am alone to blame, in perhaps expecting too much in its prowess and valor."

Lee withdrew his decimated army to the Rappahannock country, destroying the Orange and Alexandria Railroad as he retired. Revealing to his wife that the wretched condition of the army had reduced his moves to defensiveness now, he wrote, "General Meade, I believe, is repairing the railroad and I presume will come on again. If I could only get some shoes and clothes for the army, I would save him the trouble."

LEE FACES GRANT

The critical year 1864 brought a bloody confrontation of the Civil War's two greatest generals: Lee and Grant. Transferred to Virginia after his triumphs in Mississippi and Tennessee, forty-two-year-old Grant was made general-in-chief by Lincoln on Mar. 12, 1864, Sherman succeeding him in the west. A draft of 500,000 men was begun Mar. 10, with 200,000 more Mar. 14. "I determined," Grant later wrote, "to hammer continuously against the armed forces of the enemy and his resources until by mere attrition, if in no other way, the military power of the rebellion was entirely broken." Grant would field a total of 140,000 men of all arms against Lee's 45,000. Noting the condescension of the men with Grant, one of Meade's staff officers predicted that Grant "would find Lee and the Army of Northern Virginia a different proposition from Bragg."

Lee had never known Ulysses S. Grant when he was a cadet at West Point. "Sam" Grant had been a class behind Longstreet with whom he formed a lasting friendship. Though his career at the academy had been rather undistinguished, Grant had won the admiration of many Southerners for his fine horsemanship. Several years after the Mexican War, Grant dropped out of the regular army. Lee knew almost nothing about his new opponent as a soldier. In the west "Unconditional Surrender" Grant's chief characteristics as a general were his pugnacity and stubborness.

In May of 1864 Grant drove at Lee with enormous superiority in numbers, armaments, and cavalry. On May 4 the Federal army began moving across the Rapidan River, and for two days a battle raged with heavy losses on both sides. Lee forced Grant from his direct line of march into The Wilderness where the fighting was bloody and the going was slow. At a critical moment in the battle Lee was again deprived of the services of his principal and most competent commander when Longstreet was wounded, shot, like Jackson, by his own men.

Lee saw that the latest Union commander, like his predecessors, gave him nothing to fear in terms of brilliant generalship. But as Grant had underestimated him, Lee underestimated the power of recovery of the new Army of the Potomac when commanded by a general as belligerently tenacious as Grant. And as Grant had no experience against an army as bold and as skillful as Lee's, Lee had no experience against an opponent who took no account of his losses and just kept coming on again and again.

Undeterred by his high losses, with the absolute will to win regardless of cost, Grant launched massive attacks. Although unsuccessful tactically, they carried him nearer and nearer to Richmond while taking a high toll of Lee's dwindling army. By constantly moving in force by Lee's right flank, Grant slowly forced the Confederate army back through Spotsylvania Court House May 10, across the North Anna River May 19 to Cold Harbor June 3 on the north side of Richmond. Failing to take Richmond by direct assault, Grant shifted his army across the James River thirty miles below Richmond to Petersburg, a vital rail junction south of the Confederate capital. Lee managed to keep his army between Grant and Richmond, but the fatal trap had been sprung. Lee was locked in the Richmond defenses. Here the situation was stabilized and Grant settled down to a siege of attrition to erode Lee's army of its remaining strength.

'A MERE QUESTION OF TIME'

The defensive moves employed by Lee against Grant during the campaign were flawless. He predicted and counteracted each of Grant's thrusts, masterfully using his interior lines of defense to maximum advantage. And his earthworks and gun emplacements were so skillfully spaced that "he elevated axe and spade to near-equal with musket and howitzer." Beginning at Spotsylvania Court House, Lee had nullified Grant's numbers by using his engineering experience to erect fortifications that were in advance of any field works previously seen in warfare. At Petersburg Lee extended the field fortifications into permanent lines that presaged trench warfare. While Lee's lines enabled him to withstand Grant's siege of the two cities from late June 1864 to Apr. 1, 1865, once his mobile army was reduced to static defense, Lee said the end would be "a mere question of time." And now Longstreet lay wounded, Jackson was dead, and his beloved Jeb Stuart, his favorite West Point cadet, had been killed early in the campaign.

With all of Lee's masterful strategic plans and brilliant tactical execution, with all of his near-magic successes throwing back overwhelming numbers of the enemy, by the fourth year of the war the North possessed the one weapon against which Lee was powerless—*starvation*. As soon as Grant began digging in at Petersburg, Lee wrote Davis, "I think it is his purpose to compel the evacuation of our present position by cutting off supplies, and that he will not renew his attempt to drive us away by force."

As the *Times* of London reported the standoff of the two contending armies at this juncture, "The Federals, willing to wound, and yet afraid to strike; the Confederates, satisfied to repel attack, yet indisposed to assume the offensive."

In a letter to his wife Lee showed that he still retained his old sense of humor. "I saw some gentlemen from Fredericksburg today," he wrote, "who said that everyone is delighted that Grant is down here and that things in the upper country are flourishing and people reviving. Grant seems so pleased with his present position that I fear he will never move again."

Now it appeared that Lee had accepted the approaching climax of the deadly and destructive drama playing itself out with a certain peace of soul and calmness. His sense of duty, honor, and country remained bright and untarnished. He had done his best. The one thought that never entered his mind, however, was that he alone, personifying as he did the heart and soul of Southern resistance, was the primary factor in prolonging the war with the United States. His soldiers still believed in him, believed that he still believed in ultimate victory. But a keen observer could see through the fatalistic facade. "His countenance," Lee was described, "seldom, if ever, exhibited the least traces of anxiety, but was firm, hopeful, and encouraged those around him in the belief that he was still confident of success. . . . It must have been the sense of having done his whole duty, and having expended on the cause every energy of his whole being, which enabled him to meet the approaching catastrophe with a calmness which seemed to those around him almost sublime."

His sense of humor, his wit, were even sharper now. Commenting on newspaper criticism, he told a friend in mock seriousness, "We made a great mistake in the beginning of our struggle. And I fear in spite of all we can do, it will prove to be a fatal mistake. We appointed all our worst generals to command our armies and all our best generals to edit the newspapers." Explaining that he had made campaign plans that appeared perfect, but the actual battles developed defects, he noted, "I occasionally wondered why I did not see some of the defects in advance. When it was all over, I found, by reading a newspaper, that these best editor-generals saw all the defects plainly from the start. Unfortunately, they did not communicate their knowledge to me until it was too late."

On Sept. 2 Sherman's troops marched into the burning city of Atlanta. The elated reaction in the North instantly removed the possibility of the Democrats winning on a peace program in the November elections. In mid-November Sherman cut his never-to-be-forgotten destructive fifty-mile swath in his famous March Through Georgia, entering Savannah on Dec. 21. By mid-February the end was approaching rapidly, Sherman now thrusting against only token opposition in South Carolina.

Lee was approached by some of his officers and members of the government on the subject of surrendering the Confederacy while its armies were still in the field in the hope of obtaining more favorable terms in a peace settlement. Lee was asked to confer with President Davis, but could not persuade himself that it was the proper province of a soldier to recommend political action. Once again he found himself facing a dilemma as to the nature of his duty. Was his duty to the constituted authority who legally represented the collapsing country? Or was it to his soldiers who looked to him for leadership?

Longstreet, on the line facing Union general Ord, had already opened the door a crack for possible negotiations. On March 2, 1865, with Davis acquiescing, even though the President did not believe anything would come of it, Lee wrote a carefully worded letter to

General Grant suggesting a meeting to discuss "a satisfactory adjustment of the present unhappy difficulties by means of a military convention. . . ." In declining to meet with Lee, Grant explained, "I have no authority to accede to your proposition for a meeting on the subject proposed. Such authority is vested in the President of the United States alone." Now Lee knew his only remaining choice as a soldier, as he wrote to his wife, was to "fight to the last."

TWILIGHT AND APPOMATTOX

Grant knew that Lee's lines were no more than an eggshell now. Sometime after midnight April 1-2 the Federal guns began to roar, keeping up a steady bombardment of the Confederate works all night while the Union infantry formed for a dawn attack. Next morning, the far right of Lee's thin grey line finally gave way under massive Federal pressure. Looking defiantly at the advancing blue lines that had penetrated his thin defenses, Lee turned to a staff officer and said, "Well, Colonel, it has happened as I told them it would at Richmond. The line has been stretched until it is broken." Then he turned Traveller about and the group moved away at the walk. This was the beginning of the end.

Under a steady Federal pounding and numerically superior pressure, Lee was forced to evacuate Petersburg, then uncover Richmond and start west. Whether he ever truly believed he could effect a link-up with Johnston we will never know, but this was his avowed plan. The movement west could not be called a retreat. Nor was it a rout. It was more like the week-long bleeding death throes of a fatally wounded animal. Men fell from hunger. Animals dropped in their traces. Units simply dissolved, ceased to exist. Nearing Appomattox Court House on Apr. 9, Lee's way was finally blocked by vastly superior Federal forces.

At three in the morning, after a couple of hours sleep, Lee began to dress in his finest uniform. To a surprised staff officer he explained, "I have probably to be Grant's prisoner, and I thought I must make my best appearance." Reports from the front confirmed the fact that the Army of Northern Virginia—what was left of it——was indeed trapped. "Then there is nothing left for me but to go and see General Grant," Lee said with anguish, adding, "and I would rather die a thousand deaths." At the thought of surrender,

Lee's courage seemed to give way a little and he was nearly unmanned. Dying "a thousand deaths" was not mere rhetoric. "How easily I could get rid of all this and be at rest," he continued. I have only to ride along the line and all will be over." Then after a long moment he added, "But it is our duty to live. What will become of the women and children of the South, if we are not here to protect them?"

The scene that followed in the parlor of the McLean house at Appomattox has become a vivid, deeply emotional drama touching the vital sinews of every American. Lee, tall, straight, stately, majestic, magnificent in his resplendent full-dress uniform, wearing his jewel-studded sword over a bright red sash. Grant, plain-looking, five feet eight, with slouched shoulders underneath his un-buttoned private's blouse spattered with mud. But equally magnificent in simple dignity at this historic juncture in the bloody Brothers War, trying to make the ordeal as easy as possible for Lee, "his feelings sad and depressed at the downfall of a foe who had fought so long and valiantly. . . ." First some small talk to break the ice about the old days in the Old Army. Then Grant scribbling the surrender terms—officers and men paroled . . . arms and material surrendered . . . officers to keep their sidearms . . . then an added statement in response to the entreaty he could see in Lee's eyes-—let all men who own a horse or a mule take them home with them to work their little farms. . . . "This will do much towards conciliating our people," Lee responded with relief. Grant paused a moment after writing and took a long look at Lee's sword. Later he explained that he thought it would have brought a needless humiliation during the terrible ordeal to have demanded it.

The historic meeting was now concluded. A bleeding nation, brought to its knees—thousands upon thousands of its sons, North and South, never to see tomorrow—must now begin to bind up its deep and awful wounds. Lee stood up and shook hands with Grant, bowed to the rest, and left the room with staff officer Marshall behind him. He crossed the porch and descended to the lowest step. Grant and his party came quietly to the porch behind Lee. Gazing across the valley toward where his bleeding army lay, an indescribable look of agony on his face, Lee thrice struck a fist slowly into the palm of his gauntleted hand, oblivious of the Federal soldiers in the courtyard who rose respectfully as he appeared. As Lee swung slowly into the saddle, his eyes brushed Grant's party on the porch.

Grant impulsively advanced, raising his hat in the Old Army salute, as the rest of his officers followed his courtesy. Lee slowly lifted his grey hat to return the salute and then walked Traveller out of the courtyard to the road. As bedlam broke loose, Grant ordered the clamor to cease. This was not a celebration; it was a requiem. "The war is over," Grant bellowed. "The Rebels are our countrymen again."

Grant not only rushed rations to the half-starved Confederate troops, but allowed them free transportation home. Friendly comraderie was shown by the officers of both sides. As Confederate General Gordon reported, "Courtesy, and even deference, were shown to the defeated officers." General Meade rode out to meet Lee, doffed his cap in the Old Army salute, and said, "Good morning, General." Lee tipped his hat and good-naturedly inquired, "What are you doing with all that grey in your beard?" "You have to answer for most of it," Meade responded cheerfully.

TIME TO HEAL THE WOUNDS

Most know Robert E. Lee only as the "Rebel General." Yet Lee's greatest and finest contribution to his country—the reunited Union—came after Appomattox. For the remaining five years of his life Lee worked tirelessly in the vanguard of the fight for peace, unity, and the rebuilding of a "New South." Yet all these major achievements are the things by which Lee is least remembered!

When the fighting ended, a physically and emotionally exhausted Lee's greatest wish was to resume life as a private citizen. Although he was prematurely old, his heart heavy with sorrow, the Southern people never did let him fulfill this wish. And once again Lee willingly followed his duty in peace as in war as an example and a leader. For Robert E. Lee was truly the symbol of the South.

"In years when ministers of God, high officials, reproachless idealists, and crusading journalists daily denounced him and his fellow Southerners, urging that he be punished for 'the sins of the South,' . . . and with his own name defamed, his motives impugned, and living with a treason indictment hanging over his head . . . Lee never passed judgment on a single person living or dead." On the contrary. He urged the Southern people to work for "the allayment of passion, the dissipation of prejudice . . . bearing in contention with the war." Lee held an abiding faith in the sense of justice of the American people and he knew that truth must ultimately prevail.

As the leader in working toward a "New South," in peace as in war his plans were not pie-in-the-sky dreams, but practical programs directed at the immediate objectives of rebuilding, where war had left just devastation, and restoring the economy of the South through the introduction of modern technological methods. Most of all he worked towards convincing farmers and plantation owners to break with their reliance on negro labor, believing it was vital for the white man to do his own work.

But for Lee and the South only the guns had ceased firing. The war went on in the form of political subjugation and financial exploitation of a people crushed by the overwhelming force of arms. Following the surrender, Lee was as unprepared as any other Southerner for the North's program of "Reconstruction" aimed at reducing the South to "an appendage of the North," and his voice calling for the building of a "New South" was largely drowned out by the convulsive upheaval during this "Age of Hate." When "Reconstruction" was finally over, a minority report of the Congressional committee investigating conditions in the South stated, "When the corruption, distortion, and villainy of the government which Congress has set up and maintained over the Southern states are thoroughly understood, as we trust they will be some day, the world will be amazed at the long-suffering and endurance of that people."

PROGRESSIVE EDUCATOR

Following the fall of the Confederacy, Lee received many lucrative offers in industry and elsewhere. Turning them all down, in October of 1865 he chose to accept the post of president of Washington College, a small, impoverished college in Lexington, Virginia, at a salary of $2,500 a year. From the day he began his duties in this new office, reporting promptly for work at 8:00 o'clock in the morning six days a week, Lee dispelled any notion that the retired general was there to serve merely as a figurehead. As one of the professors wrote, "He had from the beginning of his presidency a distinct policy and plan which he had fully perceived and to which he steadily adhered, so that all his particular measures of progress were but consistent steps in its development. His object was nothing less than to establish and perfect an institution which should meet the highest needs of education in every department." Today, Washington and Lee University, and its many outstanding graduates over the past hundred years, attest to the success of Lee's untiring efforts from 1865 to 1870.

Here for the next five years, as a surprisingly progressive educator, Lee labored to build up the school and to unify his country. By employing his lifelong practices in economy, he soon placed the institution on a sound basis and awakened in his students —many of them veterans of the recent war—the desire to rebuild their state with the goal of good citizenship in a nation that in time would become reunited once again in heart and spirit as well as politically. Lee never ceased to do everything in his power to promote nationalism and brotherhood at a time when sectionalism and the bitterness of Reconstruction were prevailing.

The results of Lee's efforts showed almost immediately. Only about fifty students were in residence at the college when Lee began. Quickly, the number swelled to double, passing the peak of prewar enrollment. Soon this number doubled, then doubled again. By 1868 almost three-quarters of the students came from outside Virginia. These included not just the states that formed the Confederacy, but New York, New Jersey, Massachusetts, Ohio, Illinois, the District of Columbia, and one from Mexico. The Prussian Consul in New Orleans even sent his two sons to college there in 1867. Everybody wanted to come to "Lee College." Lee never ran Washington College as a "military" school. On the contrary. He used the same technique he had employed with cadets when he was Commandant of West Point. He placed them on their own responsibility and their honor as gentlemen. He believed that education depended as much on character as learning.

Lee became a familiar figure in Lexington, and every school-child knew him. An intimate glimpse is caught of the old soldier standing in a blacksmith shop watching the smithy put new shoes on Traveller. When sparks lurched from the bellows, the big horse shied and the blacksmith looked questioningly at Lee. The old Confederate reassured the smithy that it was alright to proceed. "He is just a little nervous," Lee explained gravely. "He has been through a lot."

'STRIKE THE TENT'

From the time Lee arrived in Lexington his physical decline began to accelerate markedly. By 1869, with snow-white hair and beard, he looked like a very old man. Yet he was still only sixty-two. On Sept. 28, 1870, returning from church, Lee took his regular place at the head of the table. He stood to say grace, but no words came. Neither puzzled nor agitated, he sat back down in his chair, and his countenance took on a look of sublime resignation. Ordered to bed by his doctors, he never smiled and only spoke in monosyllables to answer questions during his relatively short confinement. When his son Custis tried to cheer him up, making the usual reference to his quick recovery, Lee only shook his head slowly from side to side and pointed his finger toward heaven.

Lee kept control of his mental powers until next to the last day, when it became obvious he was sinking. In his mind, as he mumbled, he was in the midst of battle again. "Tell Hill he must come up," came the clear command. Then he lapsed into unconsciousness. During his final delirium, his last clear words were a prophetic, "Strike the tent." And on the morning of Oct. 12, 1870 he gave one deep sigh and as his wife told it, "at last sank to rest."

APPOMATTOX COURT HOUSE

HEADQUARTERS ARMY NORTHERN VIRGINIA,
APRIL 10TH 1865.

AFTER FOUR YEARS OF ARDUOUS SERVICE, MARKED BY UNSURPASSED COURAGE AND FORTITUDE, THE ARMY OF NORTHERN VIRGINIA HAS BEEN COMPELLED TO YIELD TO OVERWHELMING NUMBERS AND RESOURCES. I NEED NOT TELL THE SURVIVORS OF SO MANY HARD FOUGHT BATTLES, WHO HAVE REMAINED STEADFAST TO THE LAST, THAT I HAVE CONSENTED TO THIS RESULT FROM NO DISTRUST OF THEM; BUT FEELING THAT VALOR AND DEVOTION COULD ACCOMPLISH NOTHING THAT COULD COMPENSATE FOR THE LOSS THAT WOULD HAVE ATTENDED THE CONTINUATION OF THE CONTEST, I HAVE DETERMINED TO AVOID THE USELESS SACRIFICE OF THOSE WHOSE PAST SERVICES HAVE ENDEARED THEM TO THEIR COUNTRYMEN. BY THE TERMS OF THE AGREEMENT, OFFICERS AND MEN CAN RETURN TO THEIR HOMES AND REMAIN THERE UNTIL EXCHANGED. YOU WILL TAKE WITH YOU THE SATISFACTION THAT PROCEEDS FROM THE CONSCIOUSNESS OF DUTY FAITHFULLY PERFORMED, AND I EARNESTLY PRAY THAT A MERCIFUL GOD WILL EXTEND TO YOU HIS BLESSING AND PROTECTION. WITH AN UNCEASING ADMIRATION OF YOUR CONSTANCY AND DEVOTION TO YOUR COUNTRY, AND A GRATEFUL REMEMBRANCE OF YOUR KIND AND GENEROUS CONSIDERATION OF MYSELF, I BID YOU AN AFFECTIONATE FAREWELL.

[SIGNED] R. E. LEE,
GENERAL